This activity
book belongs to ...

----

77 Bible Activities for Kids

Copyright © 2019 by Christian Art Kids,
an imprint of Christian Art Publishers,
PO Box 1599, Vereeniging, 1930, RSA

© 2019
First edition 2019

Designed by Christian Art Kids

Images used under license from Shutterstock.com

Scripture quotations are taken from the *Holy Bible*, Contemporary English Version®. Copyright © 1995 by American Bible Society. All rights reserved.

Scripture quotations are taken from the *Holy Bible*, English Standard Version. Copyright © 2001 by Crossway Bibles, a publishing ministry of Good News Publishers. Used by permission. All rights reserved.

Scripture quotations are taken from the *Holy Bible*, International Children's Bible Copyright © 1986, 1988, 1999, 2015 by Tommy Nelson™, a division of Thomas Nelson. Used by permission.

Scripture quotations are taken from the *Holy Bible*, New International Version® NIV®. Copyright © 1973, 1978, 1984, 2011 by International Bible Society. Used by permission of Biblica, Inc.® All rights reserved worldwide.

Scripture quotations are taken from the *Holy Bible*, New Living Translation, copyright © 1996, 2004, 2007, 2013, 2015 by Tyndale House Foundation. Used by permission of Tyndale House Publishers, Carol Stream, Illinois 60188. All rights reserved.

Printed in China

ISBN 978-1-4321-3078-7

21 22 23 24 25 26 27 28 29 30 – 14 13 12 11 10 9 8 7 6 5

Printed in Shenzhen, China
OCTOBER 2021
Print Run: PUR401900

God Made Me Special

My name is:

_____

This is me

Paste your photo here

My favorite food is:

favorite color is:

This is something I love to do:

I Love Jesus!}

The Bible

Fill in the missing names of the books of the Bible

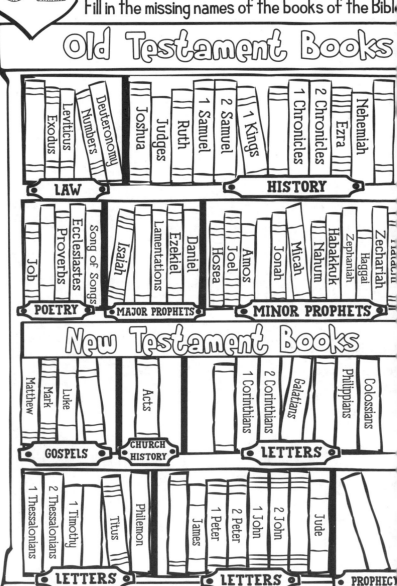

Old Testament Books

LAW
Exodus, Leviticus, Numbers, Deuteronomy

HISTORY
Joshua, Judges, Ruth, 1 Samuel, 2 Samuel, 1 Kings, 1 Chronicles, 2 Chronicles, Ezra, Nehemiah

POETRY
Job, Proverbs, Ecclesiastes, Song of Songs

MAJOR PROPHETS
Isaiah, Lamentations, Ezekiel, Daniel

MINOR PROPHETS
Hosea, Joel, Amos, Jonah, Micah, Nahum, Habakkuk, Zephaniah, Haggai, Zechariah

New Testament Books

GOSPELS
Matthew, Mark, Luke

CHURCH HISTORY
Acts

LETTERS
1 Corinthians, 2 Corinthians, Galatians, Philippians, Colossians

LETTERS
1 Thessalonians, 2 Thessalonians, 1 Timothy, Titus, Philemon

LETTERS
James, 1 Peter, 2 Peter, 1 John, 2 John, Jude

PROPHECY

Creation

03

Color the picture of the earth
and draw a sun, the moon,
and some stars.

In the beginning God
created the heavens
and the earth.

Genesis 1:1

Birds in the Bible

Circle the birds that appear in the Bible.
Cross out the ones that don't.

So God created every winged bird according
to its kind. And God saw that it was good.

Genesis 1:21

Flamingo

Sparrow

Eagle

Dove

Swan

Rooster

Raven

Duck

Swallow

Clue: Genesis 8:8, Isaiah 40:31, I Kings 17:6, Matthew 26:34, Psalm 84:3

Noah Builds an Ark

"So make yourself an ark of cypress wood.
I am going to bring floodwaters on the earth."
Genesis 6:14, 17

How many of the following tools are there?

| PLANKS | AXES | NAILS | HAMMERS |

God's Creatures

See if you can think of an animal, bird, insect or fish fr▪
A–Z. If you get stuck, ask your mom or dad for help▪

A _____

B _____

C _____

D _____

E _____

F _____

G _____

H _____

I _____

J _____

K _____

L _____

M _____

N _____

O _____

P _____

Q _____

R _____

S _____

T _____

U _____

V _____

W _____

X _____

Y _____

Z _____

God Made the Animals

God said, "I command the earth to give life to all kinds of tame animals, wild animals, and reptiles."

Genesis 1:24

Match the animal with its shadow.

Two by Two

"You are to bring into the ark two of all living creatures, male and female."

Genesis 6:19

Unscramble the words below to find the name of an animal.

bitbar _____

irteg _____

danap _____

lnio _____

mykone _____

tanpheel _____

he Animals Find Noah

There will be two of every kind of bird,
nimal and crawling thing. They will come
o you to be kept alive." Genesis 6:20

09

elp the animals
et to the ark.

Noah's Dove Returns

Then Noah sent out a dove. This was to find out if the water had dried up from the ground.

Genesis 8:8

A   B   C   Which path should the dove follow to find a branch?

God's Rainbow Promise

Color by numbers.

2- Orange   3- Yellow   4- Green   5- Blue   6- Indigo   7- Violet

I am putting **MY RAINBOW** in the **CLOUDS.** It is the sign
of the agreement between me and the earth.
When I bring clouds over the earth,
rainbow appears in the clouds.
Then I will remember my agreement.
Floodwaters will never again destroy
all life on the earth.

Genesis 9:13-15

Abraham Obeys God

"Through your descendants all the nations
on the earth will be blessed,
because you obeyed Me."

Genesis 22:18

Fill up the sky with stars and make as many dots of sand as you car
the seashore. Now think of the vastness of the night sky and the g
of sand on the beach – we can't even imagine how many there ar
God promised that Abraham's descendants would be that many.

A Robe of Many Colors

One day Jacob had a special gift made for Joseph— a beautiful robe.

Genesis 37:3

Color the robe by the numbers.

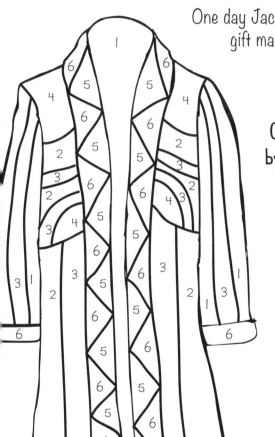

1- Purple

2- Green

3- Blue

4- Red

5- Orange

6-Yellow

Joseph's Silver Cup

My master has been good to you. So why
have you stolen his silver cup?

Genesis 44:4

Spot the odd one out.

Joseph and His Brothers

You meant to hurt me. But God turned your evil into good. It was to save the lives of many people.

Genesis 50:20

Cross out the following letters on the pyramid and see what Joseph did to his brothers.

T, H, A, U, L, M, K, N.

Escape from Egypt

The Lord made the sea become dry ground.
The water was split. And the Israelites
went through the sea on dry land.
A wall of water was on both sides.

Exodus 14:21-22

Arrange the pictures in the correct order.

Clues: Exodus 3:1-17, Exodus 7-11, Exodus 14, Exodus 20

Moses and the Burning Bush

God said, "Do not come any closer.
Take off your sandals. You are standing on holy ground."

Exodus 3:5

Connect the dots.

The Ten Commandments

Then God gave the people all these instructions:

Exodus 20:

Put the missing words in the correct place. Look at the numbers to help you.

1. You must not have any other ___ but Me.

2. You must not make for yourself an ____.

3. You must not _____ the name of the Lord your God.

4. Remember to keep the _____ holy.

5. Honor your _____.

6. You must not _____ anyone.

7. You must not commit _____.

8. You must not _____.

9. You must not ___.

10. Do not _____.

7- adultery   1- god   3- misuse   6- murder   4- Sabbath
8- steal   2- idol   9- lie   5- parents   10- covet

The Life of Moses

Find the words that refer to Moses'
life story in the word search.

basket, Nile, Egypt, staff, Pharaoh, plague,
Passover, lamb, desert, law, Aaron

A	B	A	S	K	E	T	M	P	P
L	M	P	L	A	G	U	E	H	K
A	A	R	O	N	Y	O	P	A	O
M	Z	N	E	M	P	K	J	R	Y
B	Q	I	L	B	T	Y	U	A	H
U	G	L	A	W	M	R	V	O	G
K	L	E	S	T	A	F	F	H	M
H	J	K	D	E	S	E	R	T	G
M	P	A	S	S	O	V	E	R	N

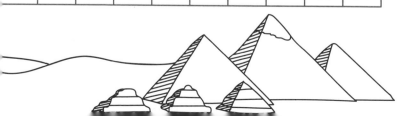

Jacob's Dream

Jacob dreamed that there was a ladder resting
on the earth and reaching up into heaven.
Genesis 28:12

Add more angels going up and down the ladder.

Rahab and the Spies

Rahab said to the Israeli spies, "Go into the hills.
The king's men will not find you there".

Joshua 2:16

Help the spies to escape
from Jericho by heading to the hills.

The Walls of Jericho Are Destroyed

When the priests blew the trumpets, the people shouted. At the sound of the trumpets and the people's shout, the walls fell. And everyone ran straight into the city.

Joshua 6:20

Write what Joshua is Saying after he saw these huge walls fall down with trumpets and shouting.

Samson's Riddle

True or false

1. Samson was in love with Delilah.   TRUE \ FALSE

2. Samson found honey in the body of a lion.   TRUE \ FALSE

3. The secret to Samson's strength was his hair.   TRUE \ FALSE

4. No one has ever been able to solve Samson's riddle.   TRUE \ FALSE

5. Samson caught 300 foxes.   TRUE \ FALSE

See the following verses for the answers

1 - Judges 16:4
2 - Judges 14:8
3 - Judges 16:17
4 - Judges 14:18
5 - Judges 15:4

24

Ruth and Naomi

Your people will be my people.
Your God will be my God.

Ruth 1:16

Help Ruth and Naomi
get to Bethlehem by
finding the path that
adds up to 10.

avid finds His Brothers

avid took the food for his brothers and left as
Jesse his father had told him.

1 Samuel 17:20

Help David to find his brothers
by following the alphabet path.

→ | A | B | C | O | P | L | B |

| B | W | B | C | F | G | M | K | N |

| C | Y | E | D | E | H | I | J | G |

| R | B | H | Q | N | M | L | K | S |

| S | R | Q | P | O | N | H | J | P |

| T | S | K | V | U | Y | Z | D | B |

| G | T | U | X | Y |

| B | H | V | W | Z |

David and Goliath

David defeated the Philistine
with only a sling and a stone!
1 Samuel 17:50

Which stone leads to Goliath?

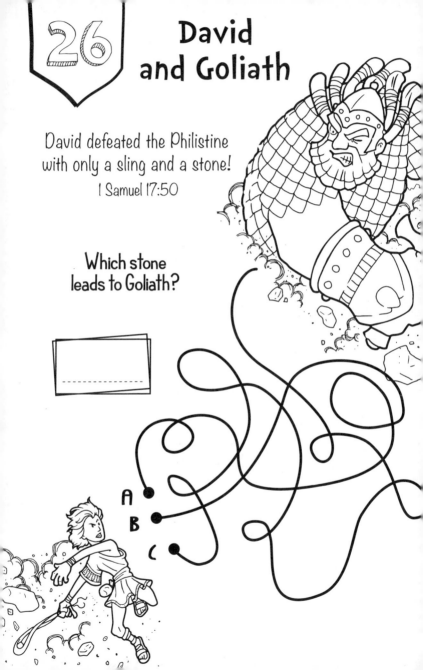

A
B
C

True Friendship

Jonathan liked David so much that they
promised to always be loyal friends.
1 Samuel 18:3

nd the words in the word jumble that describe good friends.

A real friend will be more loyal than a brother.
Proverbs 18:24

G	B	Y	L	K	E	T	M	R	P
E	P	O	S	I	T	I	V	E	A
N	A	L	H	N	Y	O	P	S	T
E	T	F	E	D	P	K	J	K	I
R	I	U	L	O	Y	A	L	Q	E
G	E	N	E	R	O	U	S	C	N
K	L	E	S	H	O	N	E	S	T
R	E	S	P	E	C	T	F	U	L
M	F	O	R	G	I	V	I	N	G

yal, respectful, patient, kind, fun, forgiving, positive, honest, generous

God Looks After Elijah

So Elijah did as the Lord told him and camped beside Kerith Brook, east of the Jordan. The ravens brought him bread and meat each morning and evening, and he drank from the brook.

1 Kings 17:5-6

Help the raven to get food to Elijah.

Elijah Hears God Speak

God can speak to us in different ways. Sometimes it is not in the loud way we expect, but in a gentle, simple way.

Read the story and place these in the correct order: whisper, earthquake, wind, fire.

First Elijah saw a _____

Then there was a _____

After the _____ there was a _____

1 Kings 19:11-13

Trees of the Bible

Crack the code to see the names of the trees in these verses.

1.
God said His people will be like great 🐾 🍎 🗝 ❄ _____

that the Lord has planted for His own glory. Isaiah 61:3

2.
I am like an 🐾 🍃 ⬆ 🐟 ✉ _____ tree growing

in God's Temple. I trust God's love forever and ever. Psalm 52:8

3.
The godly will flourish like 🦋 🍎 🍃 🎵 _____ tree

and grow strong like the ☎ ✉ 🔁 🍎 🌂 ❄ _____

of Lebanon. Psalm 92:12

4.
Elijah came to a 🦋 🌂 🐾 🐾 🎵 _____ bush, sat down

under it and prayed. Then he lay down under the bush and

fell asleep. All at once an angel touched him. 1 Kings 19:5

5.
The stork's home is in the 🌸 ⬆ 🌂 _____ trees.

Psalm 104:17

A	B	C	D	E	F	G	H	I	J	K	L	M
🍎	🦋	☎	🔁	✉	🌸	👣	♡	⬆	🐞	🗝	🍃	🎵

N	O	P	Q	R	S	T	U	V	W	X	Y	Z
📓	🐾	✈	🔔	🌂	❄	🔧	🛡	🐟	🕐	★	🌷	⌐

The Widow's Oil

Her sons kept bringing jars to her, and she filled one after another. Soon every container was full to the brim! "Bring me another jar," she said to one of her sons. "There aren't any more!" he told her. And then the olive oil stopped flowing.

2 Kings 4:5-6

How many jars can you count?

God can easily turn the little you have into a lot!

A Young King

Fill in the missing words

King _____ was _____ years old

when he became king. He was a _____ king.

| good | Josiah | eight |

Join the dots to see what a king wears.

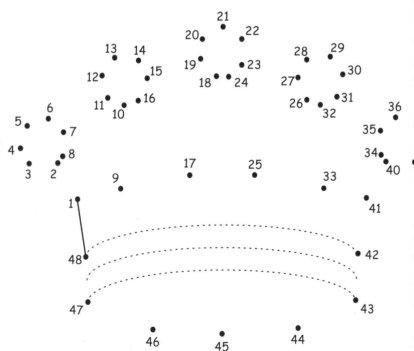

My Thank You Alphabet

Think of something you are grateful for – from A to Z.

A _____

B _____

C _____

D _____

E _____

F _____

G _____

H _____

I _____

J _____

K _____

L _____

M _____

N _____

O _____

P _____

Q _____

R _____

S _____

T _____

U _____

V _____

W _____

X _____

Y _____

Z _____

Rebuilding the Wall

I was inspecting the walls of Jerusalem.
They had been broken down.
And the gates had been destroyed by fire.
Nehemiah 2:15, 17

Nehemiah had to rebuild the walls of Jerusalem, but the walls were destroyed. With God's help, Nehemiah fixed the very big, long and thick walls in only 52 days.

Fix the walls by drawing the bricks and coloring them.

The king loved Esther more than any of the other young women. He was so delighted with her that he set the royal crown on her head and declared her queen.

Esther 2:17

Safe with God

Let all who take refuge in You rejoice.
Spread Your protection over them, that all
who love Your name may be filled with joy.

Psalm 5:11

Draw yourself under the umbrella, warm and dry.
Then draw clouds and lots of raindrops. Always remember
that you are safe under God's protection, just like an
umbrella keeps you dry from the rain.

David's Song

Use the key below to crack the code.

⟋✉ 🍃🐾🦌⇄ ⇧❄ 🎵🌷 ❄♡✉🦌♡✉🦌⇄;

- -

♡🍎🐟✉ 🍎🍃🍃 🔧♡🍎🔧 ⇧ 📓✉✉⇄.

- -

✉ 🍃✉🔧❄ 🎵✉ 🦌✉❄🔧 ⇧📓 👣🦌✉✉📓

- -

🎵✉🍎⇄🐾⏰❄.

Psalm 23:1-2

- - - - - - - - - - - - - -

	B	C	D	E	F	G	H	I	J	K	L	M
	🦋	📞	⇄	✉	⚙	👣	♡	⇧	🐞	🔑	🍃	🎵
	O	P	Q	R	S	T	U	V	W	X	Y	Z
	🐾	✈	🔔	🦌	❄	🔧	🛡	🐟	⏰	☆	🌷	➡

Lost and Found

The Lord is my shepherd.
Psalm 23:1

Help the shepherd to find his lost sheep.

The Whole World

Fill in the earth by drawing waves
in the sea and some trees on the land.
See if you can add some birds and fish.

The earth is the Lord's, and everything in it.
The world and all its people belong to Him.
Psalm 24:1

Sing to the Lord

Sing joyfully to the Lord.
Psalm 33:1

Join the dots to see who is singing a chirpy song.
Add some more music notes.

God Is Love

God, Your love is so precious!
Psalm 36:7

Color this verse and think about how much God loves you.

1 John 4:8

Sing Praises to the Lor

Let every living creature praise the Lord.
Psalm 150:6

Crack the code to see the song of praise.

_____

_____

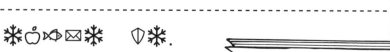

_____

Psalm 96:2

_____

A	B	C	D	E	F	G	H	I	J	K	L	M

N	O	P	Q	R	S	T	U	V	W	X	Y	Z

Powerful Proverbs

Match the pictures to the missing word in each proverb.

Kind words are like ◯
they cheer you up
and make you feel strong.
Proverbs 16:24

◯ don't have leaders,
but they store up food
during harvest season.
Proverbs 6:7-8

Watch your tongue and
keep your ◯ shut, and
you will stay out of trouble.
Proverbs 21:23

The Lord is a mighty ◯
where His people
can run for safety.
Proverbs 18:10

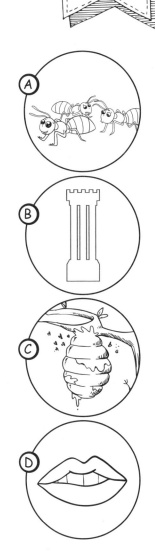

A

B

C

D

44 Think on These Things

Finally, brothers and sisters, whatever is **true**, whatever is **noble**, whatever is **right**, whatever is **pure**, whatever is **lovely**, whatever is **admirable**—if anything is **excellent** or **praiseworthy**—think about such things.

Philippians 4:8

Find the bold words in the verse
in the word search below.

B	T	E	D	E	R	X	U	W	J	O	
K	L	R	Y	X	G	I	V	A	I	L	N
O	B	M	O	U	C	J	C	G	F	H	O	W
N	N	O	B	L	E	X	Z	A	H	J	V	Q
M	B	F	X	P	L	I	Y	Q	B	T	E	Z
B	U	O	I	C	L	Q	B	U	B	Y	L	H
P	R	A	I	S	E	W	O	R	T	H	Y	E
J	Y	B	A	W	N	L	B	E	G	I	C	P
B	W	V	B	D	T	Y	U	O	H	N	Q	B
	R	D	A	D	M	I	R	A	B	L	E	Z
	B	U	L	J	S	R	A	C	D	X	

The Wisdom of Solomon

Solomon was the wisest king to ever have lived.
Break the code and memorize his wise words.

WISDOM BEGINS

WITH RESPECT FOR

THE LORD.

Proverbs 9:10

	B	C	D	E	F	G	H	I	J	K	L	M
	🦋	📞	⇄	✉	🏵	👣	♡	⇧	🐞	🔑	🍃	🎵
	O	P	Q	R	S	T	U	V	W	X	Y	Z
	🐾	✈	🔔	𓄿	❄	🔧	🛡	🐟	🕐	☆	🌷	⇨

A Strong Tower

The Lord is like a strong tower;
those who do right can run to Him for safety
Proverbs 18:10

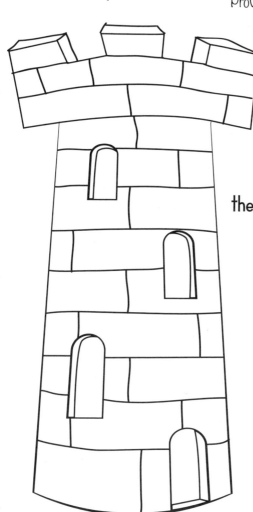

God is like a strong tower
we can run to in times
of trouble. We can be
safe with Him.

In the tower write
the different names of God.

Father

Holy One

King of kings

Creator

Almighty

Eternal One

Shield

Provider

Healthy Daniel

Daniel and his three friends looked healthier and better nourished than the young men who had been eating the food assigned by the king. So after that, the attendant fed them only vegetables.

Daniel 1:15-16

On the plate draw some healthy foods, like fruit and vegetables.

Jonah and the Whale

When I was in trouble, Lord,
I prayed to You and You listened to me.

Jonah 2:2

Connect the dots and draw Jonah in the belly of the whale.

The Lost Son

The prodigal son went home to his father.
Luke 15:20

Help the son find his way back to his father.

Numbers in the Bible

Match the sentence with the correct numb[er]

1

2

3

4

5

6

7

8

9

10

- Four friends carried their lame friend to Jesus to be healed.

- Pharaoh dreamed of seven fat cows and seven thin cows.

- The wise men brought three kinds of gifts to Baby Jesus.

- God sent ten plagues on the Egyptians.

- God made the world in six days.

- Eight people were on the ark – Noah and all his family.

- Noah took two of every kind of animal onto the ark.

- Nine lepers did not thank Jesus for healing them.

- Jesus is God's one and only Son.

- David had five stones and a sling when he went to fight Goliath.

The Word of God

Link the word with the image.

The Bible is the most important book we can ever read.
It is like a ...

COMPASS

LIGHT

SWORD

MAP

Mary's Song

Crack the code and find out what Mary said after the angel Gabriel told her that she would have a baby – Jesus!

"OH, HOW MY SOUL

PRAISES THE LORD.

HOW MY SPIRIT REJOICES

IN GOD MY SAVIOR!"

Luke 1:46-47

A	B	C	D	E	F	G	H	I	J	K	L	M
🍎	🦋	📞	⇄	✉	⚙	👣	♡	⇧	🐞	🔑	🍃	♫

N	O	P	Q	R	S	T	U	V	W	X	Y	Z
🖥	🐾	✈	🔔	🐌	❄	🔧	🛡	🐟	🕐	☆	🌷	⇥

Joseph and Mary Go to Bethlehem

While Joseph and Mary were in Bethlehem, the time came for her to have the baby.

Luke 2:6

Help Mary and Joseph to get to Bethlehem. Add the numbers of each path until you find the one which totals 10.

Three Wise Men

Guide the wise men to Baby Jesus.

The wise men saw the same star they had seen in the east.
It went before them until it stopped above
the place where the child was.

Matthew 2:9

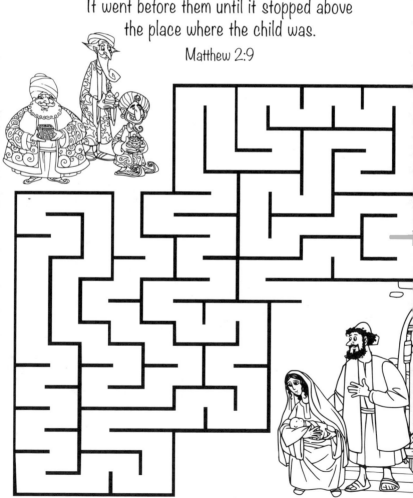

How many words can you make using the letters from CHRISTMAS? Only use the letters as many times as shown.

CHRISTMAS

Fishers of Men

"Follow Me, and I will make you become fishers of men."

Mark 1:17

How many times can you find the word FISH in the word search

	I	H	H	F						
H	F	S	I	S	F				F	
H	F	I	S	H	F	I	F		F	I
F	F	F	S	F	F	I	S	H	I	F	I	S
F	I	S	H	F	I	S	H	F	I	S	S	H
S	S	S	F	I	H	S	I	F	I	S	H	F
H	I	H	F	I	S	H	I		F	I
	F	I	S	H	I	H			S	
		S	F							

Following Jesus

ut the words in the footprints in order
o show other people that you follow Jesus.

know 4
if 10
All 1
other. 14
that 5
you 11
My 8
you 6
followers 9
are 7
each 13
will 3
love 12
people 2

John 13:35

58

Talking to God

As long as I live, I will pray to You.
Psalm 63:4

Doodle and color in the letters below
to help you remember how to pray.

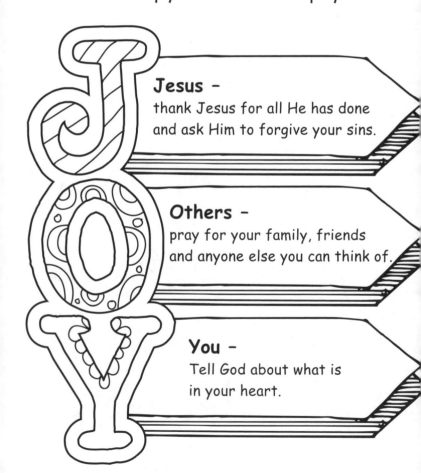

Jesus –
thank Jesus for all He has done
and ask Him to forgive your sins.

Others –
pray for your family, friends
and anyone else you can think of.

You –
Tell God about what is
in your heart.

The Lord's Prayer

In the space below, write your own prayer to God.

59

Our Father in heaven,
we pray that Your name will always be kept holy.
We pray that Your kingdom will come.
We pray that what You want will be done,
here on earth as it is in heaven.
Give us the food we need for each day.
Forgive the sins we have done,
just as we have forgiven those who did wrong to us.
And do not cause us to be tested;
but save us from the Evil One.
The kingdom, the power,
and the glory are Yours forever.

Amen

Jesus Feeds the Crowd

Jesus divided the loaves of bread. He gave them to His followers, and they gave the bread to the people. All the people ate and were satisfied.

Matthew 14:19-20

Find these faces in the crowd.

More than 5,000 people were fed with five loaves of bread and two fish on that day.

Jesus Calms the Storm

Jesus got up and ordered the wind
and the waves to be quiet. The wind stopped,
and everything was calm.

Mark 4:39

Complete the picture by drawing waves
on the sea and some fish or birds.

The Last Supper

The disciples did as Jesus told them and prepar
the Passover meal there. When it was evening,
Jesus sat down at the table with the Twelve.

Matthew 26:19-20

Find the following words in the word jumble:

bread, wine, feast, supper, table, Jesus, disciples, cup

D	B	Y	S	J	E	T	M	P	P
L	I	P	L	K	G	J	E	H	K
Q	A	S	U	P	P	E	R	T	O
M	Z	J	C	M	P	S	J	A	Y
B	W	I	L	I	T	U	U	B	H
R	G	I	A	W	P	S	V	L	G
E	L	C	N	T	Y	L	F	E	M
A	J	U	D	E	S	B	E	T	G
D	K	P	S	S	F	E	A	S	T

The Good Samaritan

he Good Samaritan took the injured man to an inn where he
could be cared for. What did he use to carry the man on?
Join the dots to find out.

Saul Sees Again

Saul has seen a vision. In it a man named Ananias comes to him and lays his hands on hi[m] Then he sees again. Acts 9:12

Lead Ananias to Saul to restore his sight.

Jesus Lives!

Christ died for us while we were still sinners.
In this way God shows His great love for us.

Romans 5:8

Use a black marker and cross out all of these letters:
T, P, A, M and O

			H	T			
			E	A			
A	P	M	P	I	S	O	P
P	O	T	R	O	P	A	M
			I	P			
			S	A			
			E	T			
			N	O			
			T	P			
			M	A			

God's Gift

Put the words in the gift boxes in order to see what free gift God has given you.

- -

- -

- -

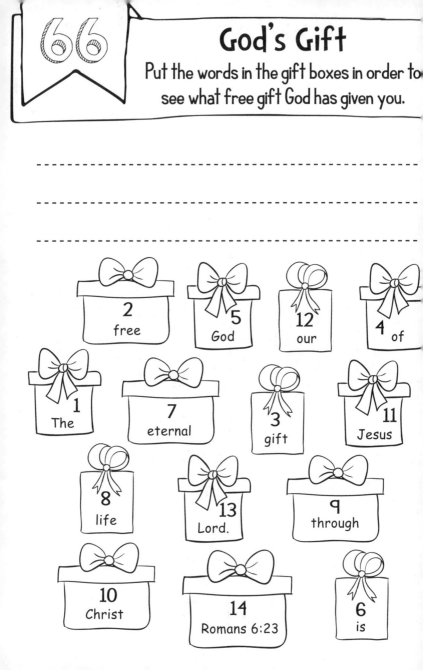

2 free

5 God

12 our

4 of

1 The

7 eternal

3 gift

11 Jesus

8 life

13 Lord.

9 through

10 Christ

14 Romans 6:23

6 is

Love Is

rite down some ways you can show your family that you love them — and then go and do it!

Love is **patient** and **kind**. Love is not jealous, it does not brag, and it is not proud. **Love** is not rude, is not selfish, and does not become angry easily. **Love** does not remember wrongs done against it. ve takes no pleasure in evil, but **rejoices** over the truth. Love patiently accepts all things. It always **trusts**, always **hopes**, and always continues **strong**. Love never ends.

1 Corinthians 13:4-8

Fruit of the Spirit

The fruit of the Spirit is ... Galatians 5:22-23

Find the fruit of the Spirit in the word search.

love, joy, peace, patience, kindness, goodness, faithfulness, gentleness, self-control.

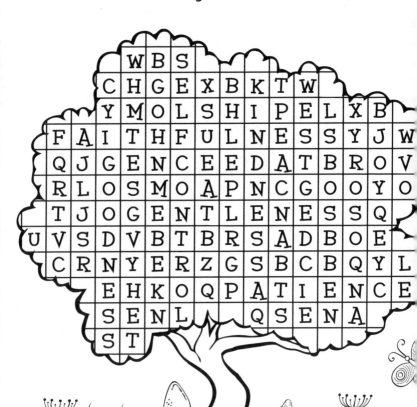

		W	B	S							
	C	H	G	E	X	B	K	T	W		
	Y	M	O	L	S	H	I	P	E	L	X	B
F	A	I	T	H	F	U	L	N	E	S	S	Y	J	W
Q	J	G	E	N	C	E	E	D	A	T	B	R	O	V
R	L	O	S	M	O	A	P	N	C	G	O	O	Y	O
T	J	O	G	E	N	T	L	E	N	E	S	S	Q
U	V	S	D	V	B	T	B	R	S	A	D	B	O	E
C	R	N	Y	E	R	Z	G	S	B	C	B	Q	Y	L
	E	H	K	O	Q	P	A	T	I	E	N	C	E
	S	E	N	L		Q	S	E	N	A
	S	T

God Loves You

We are God's masterpiece.
Ephesians 2:10

scribe or draw what you are good at or what you like about
ourself. Have you thanked God for giving you these gifts?

The Armor of God

Put on every piece of God's armor so you will be able to resist the enemy in the time of evil.

Ephesians 6:13

Link the piece of God's armor to the soldier.

Shield of Faith

Shoes of the Gospel of Peace

Breastplate of Righteousness

Sword of the Spirit

Belt of Truth

Helmet of Salvation

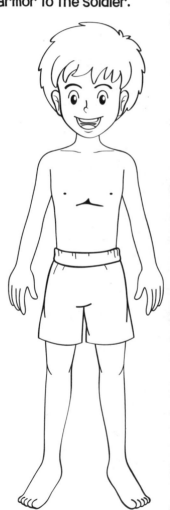

Running the Race

...un toward the goal, so that I can win the prize
...being called to heaven. This is the prize that
...offers because of what Christ Jesus has done.

Philippians 3:14

...in the dots to see what the winner of a race gets for first
...ace. The Bible says that if we live for Jesus our reward will
be to go to heaven.

72 Obey Your Parents

Children, always obey your parents,
for this pleases the Lord.

Colossians 3:20

If the behavior below is good draw a
happy emoji in the circle. If the behavior
is disobedient to your parents draw a sad
emoji in the circle.

Helping around the house

SHOUTING

Doing what you are told to do

Ignoring

Tantrums

RESPECTFUL

POLITE

Sulkin

Back-chatting

NOT SHARIN

Saying sorry

Breaking things

Jesus' Helpers

Find the names of all 12 disciples.

Peter, James the Great, John, Andrew, Philip,
Bartholomew, Matthew, Thomas, James the Less,
Thaddeus, Simon, and Judas.

B	T	E	D	E	R	X	U	W	J	O	M	B
J	A	M	E	S	T	H	E	G	R	E	A	T
B	M	R	U	C	J	C	G	F	H	O	T	B
N	O	B	T	E	X	Z	P	H	J	V	T	A
B	F	X	T	H	A	D	D	E	U	S	H	V
J	O	I	A	J	O	H	N	B	T	L	E	S
R	U	I	S	N	W	L	R	T	H	E	W	I
Y	B	D	W	N	D	B	O	G	I	C	R	M
W	V	B	A	T	Y	R	O	M	N	Q	B	O
J	A	M	E	S	T	H	E	L	E	S	S	N
H	I	L	I	P	S	R	A	W	D	W	X	H

Pray Every Day

Always be joyful and never stop praying.
1 Thessalonians 5:16-17

God loves to hear your prayers. Write a letter in each petal: PRAY Color it in. It will remind you to pray every day!

Names of Jesus

She will bear a son, and you shall call His name
Jesus, for He will save His people from their sins.

Matthew 1:21

Fill in the names
of Jesus on the cross.

Bread of Life
Good Shepherd
Lamb of God
True Vine
Savior
Living Water
Morning Star
Lord of Lords
Rock
Prince of Peace
Light of the World

A Message for You

Crack the code to discover a special message for you!

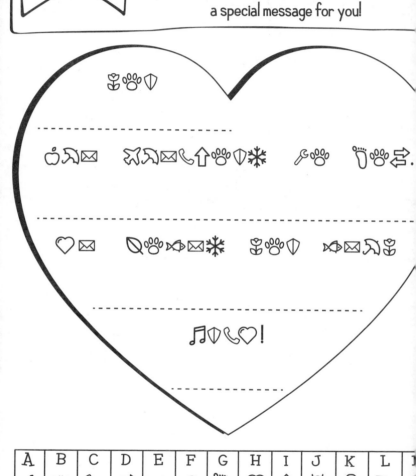

The Golden Rule

THE GOLDEN RULE

Treat others as
you want
them
to treat you.

Matthew 7:12

Treat others as you want
them to treat you.
Matthew 7:12

Cut out the bookmark
and color it in.